A ROOKIE READER

PANCAKES, CRACKERS, AND PIZZA

A BOOK ABOUT SHAPES

By Marjorie Eberts and
Margaret Gisler

Illustrations by Stephen Hayes

Prepared under the direction of Robert Hillerich, Ph.D.

SCHOLASTIC INC.

New York Toronto London Auckland Sydney
Mexico City New Delhi Hong Kong Buenos Aires

To our mothers

ISBN 0-516-24500-7

12 11 10   5 6 7/0

Printed in Mexico   61

First Scholastic printing, September 2002

This is Eddy.

Eddy likes to eat, and eat, and eat.

5

Eddy eats round things.

Eddy eats pancakes,

oranges,

and eggs.

12

Eddy eats square things.

Eddy eats crackers,

meat,

and cheese.

Eddy eats triangles.

20

Eddy eats pizza,

salad,

and watermelon.

Eddy eats circles,

and squares,

and triangles.

Eddy eats all shapes.

Eddy eats, and eats, and eats.

Eddy looks

like what he eats.

WORD LIST

		round
all	he	salad
and	is	shapes
cheese	like	square(s)
circles	likes	things
crackers	looks	this
eat	meat	to
eats	oranges	triangles
Eddy	pancakes	watermelon
eggs	pizza	what

About the Authors

Marjorie Eberts and **Margaret Gisler** have spent the last few years collaborating on books dealing with the language arts. Both have had experience as teachers and have masters degrees in reading from Butler University. This is their first Rookie Reader.

About the Artist

Stephen Hayes is a free-lance, humorous illustrator from Cincinnati, Ohio. He received his degree in Fine Arts from Miami University in Oxford, Ohio. Steve has illustrated humorous greeting cards and several books for children. This book is dedicated to his wife, Susan, and his daughter, Sarah.